You are exact

Stories of girls who d

uniqueness

Emma Lenders

You are just right

Stories of girls who discover their uniqueness

Printing and distribution by order:
Gumtamin Nutrition GmbH, Hombergen 122, 41334 Nettetal
ISBN: 978-3-68991-015-0
Year of publication: 2024

Contents

Your uniqueness makes you strong

Have you ever wondered why you're different? Maybe sometimes you feel like you don't quite fit in, like you think differently, look different or have different interests to the girls around you. This can sometimes be confusing and even scary. But you know what? It's those very differences that make you special.

This book tells stories of girls who are just like you - unique in every way. Each of these girls has learned that their uniqueness is a strength, not a weakness. They have realized that it doesn't matter how others see you, but how you see yourself. Because only you can decide who you really are and what you want to achieve.

So if you ever have doubts about yourself, if you wonder whether you are good enough, strong enough or smart enough, remember: you are exactly right the way you are. This book should encourage you to celebrate your uniqueness and be proud of what makes you who you are.

Immerse yourself in the stories of girls who go their own way, who learn to love themselves and discover their special talents and strengths. Let yourself be inspired and always remember: your uniqueness makes you strong.

Lea discovers her strength in the water

Lea stood in her room and stared in the mirror. A dark blue swimsuit hung in front of her, which normally made her feel confident and comfortable. But today everything was different. The school had announced that the annual swimming tournament would take place this week, and this time the seventh grade girls were to take part. Normally, Lea would have been thrilled - she loved swimming. But the idea of standing in front of all her classmates in a swimsuit made her feel self-conscious.

Lea was taller and stronger than most of her friends. While many girls in her class were petite and slender, Lea had an athletic, muscular build. Her shoulders were broad, her arms strong and her legs powerful - characteristics that made her the best swimmer in her class, but which also often made her feel insecure. In gym class, she was often called "strong" or "powerful", but she knew that these terms were not always meant as compliments.

"Why can't I just be like the others?" she thought, sighing softly as she pulled on her swimsuit. "Why do I have to be so big and strong?"

When she finally stood in front of the mirror, she pulled her sweater over it to cover her shoulders. "Maybe then no one will notice how broad I am," she muttered to herself. But the queasy feeling in her stomach remained as she went downstairs.

"Lea, are you ready?" her mother called from the kitchen as she heard her daughter coming down the stairs.

"Yes, Mama," Lea replied, but her voice didn't sound as cheerful as usual. She sat down at the breakfast table, but she couldn't eat anything. Her thoughts were all about the swimming tournament and the insecurity she felt inside.

"You look great," said her mother, placing a hand lovingly on Lea's shoulder. "I know you're a bit nervous, but you're a fantastic swimmer. You're going to do great."

Lea forced herself to smile, but didn't want to say anything. She didn't want to show her mother how much she was dreading the day.

At school, Lea tried to hide her insecurity, but she found it difficult. While the other girls talked and laughed happily, she stayed in the background. "What if they laugh at me?" she asked herself as they entered the swimming pool. She was afraid of how she would look in her swimsuit. "Everyone will look at me and I'll feel terrible."

"Hey, Lea!" her friend Jana called out and came up to her. "Are you ready for the tournament? It's going to be great!"

Lea smiled weakly and nodded. "Yeah, sure," she replied, although she would have liked to just run away. But she knew that she had to face this challenge, even if it was difficult.

When the tournament started, all the girls stood at the edge of the pool, ready to jump into the water. Lea could feel her heart beating faster and her hands getting clammy. "Why am I even doing this?" she asked herself. "I should just push myself."

But when the starting signal sounded and the other girls jumped into the water, something in her was awakened. Lea had always loved how it felt to be in the water. The feeling of gliding through the water was something that had always calmed her and made her happy. Now she just had to remember it.

She plucked up all her courage, took off her sweater and stood there in her swimsuit. For a moment, she had the feeling that all eyes were on her, but then she took a deep breath and jumped into the water. The coldness of the water immediately enveloped her and suddenly everything felt better.

Being in the water was something she had always loved. Here, her strong stature no longer counted as a disadvantage. On the contrary, she felt the strength of her arms and legs as they carried her through the water. With every stroke she took, she felt safer and stronger.

During the race, she concentrated only on her rhythm, on the feeling of breaking through the water. She no longer thought about the spectators, her friends or how she looked in her swimsuit. All that mattered was the swim. She could feel herself getting faster, overtaking the other girls, and with every meter she covered, her confidence grew.

When she finally reached the wall and surfaced, she heard the cheers of the spectators. Her classmates clapped enthusiastically and when she got out of the water, Jana ran towards her. "Lea, you were amazing!" she shouted and hugged her, "You won!"

Lea gasped and felt a smile spread across her face. "Thank you," she said, and for the first time that day she felt really comfortable in her skin. She had done it. Not only had she won the race, she had also overcome her insecurities.

After the tournament, Lea and her friends sat on the edge of the pool and talked about their experiences. "I always thought that my stature was a disadvantage," Lea finally confessed. "But today I realized that it helped me. I think I have to learn to accept my strength."

"Your strength makes you special," said Jana, putting her arm around Lea. "And you're an incredible swimmer."

Lea nodded and felt as if she had learned something important at that moment. Her strong physique was not something to be ashamed of - on the contrary, it made her strong and special. From now on, she would celebrate her uniqueness and no longer hide.

Lea has learned that her size and strength are not something to be ashamed of. She has discovered that these very qualities give her an advantage in the water and that they make her a great swimmer. You are unique too, and it is precisely this uniqueness that makes you special. Trust in your strengths and be proud of what makes you special - because you are just right the way you are.

You are good just the way you are.

Maja finds her true friends

Maja stood in front of the big school gate and felt her heart beating faster. It was her first day at the new school and the uncertainty weighed heavily on her shoulders. She had left her old school behind and was now starting a new chapter in her life. A chapter she didn't know what it held in store for her. The other students burst into the school laughing, while Maja hesitated at the entrance before taking a deep breath and setting off.

At her old school, Maja had had friends, people she had known for a long time and with whom she felt comfortable. But everything was different now. The school was bigger, the classrooms more labyrinthine, and the pupils... They all seemed so confident, so sure of what they were doing. Maja felt small and insecure.

During lessons, she tried to concentrate on the new subjects and teachers, but her thoughts kept wandering. "How am I going to make friends here?" she asked herself. "What if no one likes me?"

During the break, Maja stood indecisively in the school playground. The other children formed small groups, laughed and talked. Maja felt like a foreign body who didn't belong. Suddenly she noticed a group of girls standing nearby and laughing together. They seemed confident and cool, just the way Maja wanted them to be. "Maybe I should try to make friends with them," she thought and walked towards the group uncertainly.

"Hey," she said quietly as she approached. The girls turned and looked at her. For a moment, Maja felt like she was being watched under a microscope, but then one of the girls smiled.

"Hi," said the girl who was obviously the leader of the group. "You're new here, aren't you?"

Maja nodded nervously. "Yes, I'm Maja. I just wanted to... I just wanted to say hello."

The other girls looked at her before the leader spoke again. "I'm Lea, and these are my friends. If you want to join us, you'll have to try a little harder." Lea's tone was friendly, but also a little mocking.

Maja didn't know exactly what Lea meant, but she smiled bravely. "What should I do?" she asked cautiously.

Lea grinned and exchanged a quick glance with the other girls. "Well, we have our rules. You just have to be relaxed and cool, you know? Not be afraid to do things that other people aren't."

Maja nodded, although she felt even more insecure inside. "Okay," she said quietly, trying not to let it show.

Over the next few days, Maja tried to fit in with the girls. She laughed at jokes she didn't understand and pretended to be interested in things she didn't actually like. Lea and the others seemed to accept her, but Maja felt more and more uncomfortable. Every day she wondered more and more whether this was really what she wanted.

One day, when the group was standing together in the schoolyard, Lea started to make fun of another girl who was walking past them. "Look at her shoes," Lea said loud enough for the girl to hear. "How can you walk around like that?"

The other girls giggled, but Maja suddenly felt bad. She had never hurt anyone on purpose before and what Lea was doing disgusted her deeply. But she didn't want to attract attention or upset Lea, so she didn't say anything. She felt caught between her desire to belong and her own conscience.

During the next break, when the group was back together, Lea wanted Maja to make fun of another girl to prove that she was "cool enough". "Come on, Maja," urged Lea. "Say something about that one over there."

Maja felt her heart beat faster. "I don't want this," she thought, "this isn't me." But the pressure of Lea's expectant gaze and the giggling girls around her was strong.

"I... I can't do this," Maja finally said, her voice quiet and uncertain.

Lea raised an eyebrow. "What do you mean?" she asked, her voice sounding sharper now. "Don't you want to be with us?"

Maja felt a lump forming in her throat. She wanted to belong, but she knew that she would lose herself if she did. "I just don't think it's me," she finally said. Her words were quiet but firm.

Lea looked at her as if she had said something incomprehensible. "All right," she finally said, shrugging her shoulders. "If you don't want to be cool, then don't." She turned and walked off with the other girls without looking back.

Maja was left alone, the feeling of relief mixed with sadness. She had known it was wrong to behave like this just to be accepted, but the fear of being alone had almost made her betray herself.

In the days that followed, Maja stayed away from Lea's group. It hurt, but at the same time she felt free. She wanted to find friends who liked her for who she was and not because she was trying to be someone else.

One afternoon, when she was sitting alone on a bench in the park reading after school, she heard a voice next to her. "Hey, you're Maja, aren't you?"

Maja looked up and spotted a girl from her class smiling at her. "Yes, that's me," she replied cautiously.

"My name is Julia," the girl said and sat down next to her. "I've been watching you over the last few days. You've stayed away from Lea and the others. I thought that was pretty brave."

Maja blushed slightly. "I... I guess I just didn't want to pretend to be someone I'm not anymore."

Julia nodded in understanding. "I can understand that very well. I tried to fit in with that group once, but it just didn't feel right. It's much better to be yourself."

Maja felt a smile spread across her face. "Yes, I think so too."

Over the following weeks, Maja became friends with Julia and her friends. She discovered that they had a lot in common and that she felt comfortable around them. With these girls, she didn't have to pretend or be different - she could just be herself.

One day, as they sat and laughed together in the park, Maja realized that she had finally found the kind of friendships she had always wanted. They were friendships based on honesty, respect and mutual understanding.

"I'm glad I stayed away from Lea," Maja said to Julia with a smile.

"You should be," Julia replied. "You had the courage to be yourself, and that's the most important thing."

Maja has learned that it is more important to stay true to yourself than to bend yourself in order to be accepted. She has discovered that real friendships are based on honesty and mutual respect. You too should always be yourself and never give up your values just to fit in. The right friends will appreciate you for who you are - unique and valuable.

You don't have to change to be valuable.

Nina, the little mathematician

Nina sat at the back of the classroom and stared at the worksheet in front of her. On the paper were complicated mathematical equations that made her classmates shift nervously in their chairs and mumble quietly to themselves. But none of this was a problem for Nina. She loved math. The numbers and formulas were like a puzzle that she could solve, and every time she found the right solution, she felt that pleasant tingle of satisfaction.

But today Nina was not satisfied. She couldn't shake off the feeling that something wasn't right. She knew that she could do the tasks faster and better than most of her class, but that was exactly what scared her. She didn't want to stand out, she didn't want to be labeled a nerd. Over the last few weeks, she had noticed how some of her classmates looked at her when she got her work back with top marks. It wasn't a nasty look, but Nina felt that she was different from the others and that made her insecure.

While the others were still poring over the tasks, Nina put her pencil down and looked out of the window. She knew that she had already found the right answers, but she didn't want to be the first to hand in her work. "Maybe I should just pretend I haven't finished yet," she thought, nervously playing with her pen.

"Nina, do you need help?" The teacher's voice snapped her out of her thoughts. Mrs. Müller stood in front of her and looked at the almost completed worksheet.

"Um... no, thanks," mumbled Nina, trying to cover the sheet a little.

Mrs. Müller smiled kindly at her. "You've almost completed all the tasks, haven't you?"

Nina nodded shyly. She liked Mrs. Müller, but she didn't want the teacher to praise her in front of the whole class. She just wanted to be like everyone else.

"That's great, Nina," Mrs. Müller said quietly so that the others wouldn't hear. "You should be proud of your skills."

But Nina couldn't be proud. She felt uncomfortable because she was so different. While the rest of the class was still poring over the tasks, everything seemed to come far too easily to her. "What's the point of being the best at math if nobody likes me?" she asked herself sadly.

Over the next few days, Nina avoided getting too involved. She tried to work more slowly and not show how good she actually was. But the more she took herself back, the more dissatisfied she felt. She loved math, but she felt like she had to hide that love in order to be accepted.

Then came the day when Ms. Müller informed the class about an upcoming math competition. It was a school-wide competition in which teams from different classes would compete against each other. Ms. Müller divided the class into teams, and Nina was paired up with three other girls who weren't particularly enthusiastic about math.

"Oh no, we've got Nina on the team," one of the girls murmured quietly as they sat down. "Now it's going to be really tough for us."

Nina felt her cheeks grow hot. She knew that the other girls thought she was too ambitious, too perfectionist. "I'll hold back," she decided at that moment. "I don't want them to think I know everything better."

The weeks went by and the team met regularly to prepare for the competition. But every time they encountered difficulties, Nina hesitated to offer her help. She didn't want to stand out too much, didn't want to be the one who knew everything. But the more she held back, the more frustrated the other girls became. They struggled with the tasks and Nina felt that she was slowly but surely becoming alienated from her abilities.

On the day of the competition, Nina was more nervous than ever. Her teammates were quiet and tense as they took their seats in the large event room. The other teams looked confident and ready, while Nina's team shifted uneasily in their chairs.

When the competition began, the first tasks were displayed on a large screen. The clock started ticking and each team had to submit their solutions as quickly as possible. Nina's team did their best, but it wasn't long before they got into trouble.

"It's far too hard," said one of the girls, putting the pencil aside in despair. "We'll never manage it."

Nina bit her lip. She saw the tasks in front of her and knew that she knew the solutions. But she remembered the words of her teammate, who hadn't been thrilled to have her on the team. "What if they think I'm a nerd again?" she thought. "Maybe I should just keep quiet."

But when she saw her friends getting more and more desperate, she couldn't bear it any longer. She knew she had to do something. "I can't let this happen," she thought and felt something stirring inside her.

"Wait," she finally said, her voice firm and determined. "I think I know how we can solve this."

The other girls looked at her in surprise. "Really?" one of them asked hopefully.

Nina nodded and picked up the pen. "Yes, let's do it together," she said. "I'll explain it to you and then we can do it."

Over the next few minutes, Nina guided the team through the tasks, explained the solutions and helped the other girls to understand the difficult parts. She worked with focus and determination, without thinking about whether she stood out or not. All that mattered was that she was helping her team.

When the time ran out and the results were announced, Nina felt exhausted but happy. She had done her best and that was all she could do.

Finally, the winners were announced and when Nina's team was called out in second place, cheers broke out among them. "We did it!" the other girls shouted and hugged each other. "Nina, you were great!"

Nina could hardly believe it. The other girls looked at her and smiled, not with mockery, but with genuine gratitude and appreciation. "You saved us," said one of the girls and squeezed her hand.

Nina smiled back, and for the first time she felt truly comfortable in her own skin. She had used her skills to help others and was not judged for it, but celebrated. She had learned that there was nothing wrong with being good at something - on the contrary, it was a strength she could be proud of.

Nina has learned that there is nothing wrong with being good at something. She has discovered that her skills and talents should not be hidden, but celebrated. You too should be proud of what you can do and not be afraid to show it. Trust in your strengths and be proud of what makes you special - because you are just right the way you are.

your uniqueness is your strength.

Sophie finds her own voice

Sophie sat in her room and listened to the muffled sounds from the hallway. Her older sister Anna had just come home and, as always, Sophie could hear her cheerful voice and the laughter of her friends. Anna was the complete opposite of Sophie in many ways. She was sporty, popular and always the center of attention. Wherever Anna appeared, a good mood was guaranteed. Sophie, on the other hand, was rather quiet, reserved and preferred to spend her time with a book or her drawing pad.

Sophie loved her sister, but it was hard not to compare herself to her. Everything seemed to come so easily to Anna - whether in sport, at school or when dealing with others. Sophie, on the other hand, often felt insecure and shy. While Anna played volleyball outside with her friends, Sophie preferred to sit in her room and draw. She knew that her parents were proud of both daughters, but sometimes she wondered if they wished she was more like Anna.

"Why can't I be like that too?" Sophie often thought. "Why can't I be sporty and confident?"

One day, during class, Sophie's teacher, Ms. Berger, announced a new school project. "Over the next few weeks, we will be looking at the topic of art and culture," she explained. "Each of you will create your own project on this topic and present it to the class at the end of the unit."

Sophie felt her heart beat faster. Art was what she loved most. She spent hours drawing and making up stories, but she had never dared to show her work to anyone. Now that she had the opportunity to showcase her talents, she felt insecure. "What if it's not good enough?" she asked herself. "What if the others don't like it?"

Once home, Sophie retired to her room and began to work on her project. She had decided to write a story and draw illustrations to go with it. It was to be a fairytale story about a girl who lived in a world full of color and fantasy. But the more she worked on her project, the more she doubted herself.

"Anna would probably do something cool and sporty," Sophie thought. "Maybe that would have gone down better."

In the weeks that followed, Sophie observed her classmates working on their projects. Some painted pictures, others made sculptures, and still others worked on music or dance. Sophie was impressed by the talents of her classmates, but she couldn't shake off the nagging insecurity. "Maybe my project is too boring," she thought.

But despite her doubts, Sophie continued to work. She loved immersing herself in the world of her story and bringing the characters to life on paper. Her drawings became more and more detailed, her story more and more exciting. It was as if she was discovering a new side to herself, a side that was full of creativity and imagination.

As the day of the presentations approached, Sophie became more and more nervous. She knew she had to present her project in front of the whole class and the idea of speaking in front of everyone made her nervous. "I wish I was braver," she thought, "Anna wouldn't be scared."

On the day of the presentation, Sophie sat quietly in her seat and watched as one student after another went forward to present their work. The class applauded politely and Sophie could feel her nervousness growing.

Finally, it was Sophie's turn. With shaky hands, she picked up her drawings and stood in front of the class. For a moment she was tempted to just turn around and walk away, but then she remembered all the hours she had put into her project. "I've worked hard on it," she told herself. "I have to try."

Sophie began to read out her story. At first her voice was quiet and unsure, but the more she delved into the story, the stronger her voice became. She talked about the brave girl in her story who traveled through a magical world full of colors and stood her ground against all odds. As she read, she showed her drawings and suddenly the room fell silent. The class listened attentively, fascinated by the imagination and depth of her story.

When Sophie had finished, she lowered her eyes and waited for the class to react. There was silence for a moment, but then thunderous applause broke out. "That was incredible,

Sophie!" shouted a classmate. "Your story was so beautiful!"

Sophie could hardly believe it. She had expected the others to find her project boring, but instead she received praise and admiration. Her teacher, Mrs. Berger, came up to her and put a hand on her shoulder. "Sophie, you have a wonderful talent," she said warmly. "Your story and your drawings are exceptional. You should be proud of yourself."

Sophie felt her insecurities evaporate. She had found her own voice and she had realized that she didn't have to be like Anna to be special. Her creativity and imagination were her strengths, and she now knew that she didn't have to hide these talents.

Sophie has learned that she doesn't have to be like her sister to be special. Everyone has their own talents and strengths, and it's important to recognize and appreciate them. You are unique too, and your creativity and imagination are valuable gifts. Trust in your abilities and be proud of what you can do - because you are just right the way you are.

It's great to be yourself.

Anna and the Power of Silence

Anna sat alone on a bench in the schoolyard and watched her classmates laughing and talking to each other during the lunch break. She held a book in her hands, an old friend who had accompanied her through many lonely breaks. Anna liked to keep to herself. She loved immersing herself in the worlds of her books, reading and thinking. But sometimes she wished she could be as self-confident and sociable as the other children.

"Why can't I just be loud and cheerful?" she often asked herself. "Why do I always have to be so quiet?"

Anna often felt invisible. At school, she noticed how the louder children attracted the attention of the teachers, how they were the center of attention and how their opinions were always heard. Anna, on the other hand, preferred to stay in the background. She knew that her thoughts were profound and well thought out, but she was afraid that they wouldn't be heard in the noisy world of school.

One day, during class, Anna's teacher, Ms. Meier, announced a new project. "We're going to do a group project on environmental protection in the next few weeks," she explained. "Each group should develop a project that shows how we can make our school more environmentally friendly."

Anna felt a mixture of excitement and nervousness spreading through her. She was very interested in environmental issues and had lots of ideas on how to make the school more sustainable. But the idea of presenting her ideas to a group scared her. "What if they don't take me seriously?" she thought, "What if my ideas aren't good enough?"

When the groups were divided up, Anna found herself in a group with three other girls - Clara, Lisa and Johanna. All three were friendly and bright girls who Anna liked, but they were also loud and self-confident. "I probably won't be able to say much," thought Anna and sat down quietly with them.

"Okay, guys, let's brainstorm," Clara said energetically as soon as they sat down in the library. "We have to come up with a great idea to win!"

"How about we start a campaign against plastic bottles?" Lisa suggested. "That would be cool."

"Yes, or we could plant trees," Johanna added. "That would also be good for the environment."

Anna listened attentively, but she didn't feel brave enough to share her own thoughts. She had an idea that she thought was particularly important, but she was afraid that the others wouldn't like it. "Maybe I just shouldn't say anything," she thought.

But while the other girls continued to discuss, Anna realized that their ideas were becoming increasingly superficial. They were good ideas, but they only scratched the surface of the problem. Anna knew that more was needed to really make a difference.

Finally, she summoned up all her courage. "I... I have an idea," she said quietly, almost in a whisper.

The other girls fell silent and looked at her. "What's your idea, Anna?" Clara asked kindly.

Anna could feel her heart beating faster, but she forced herself to keep talking. "I've been thinking that maybe we shouldn't just talk about plastic bottles or trees. What if we develop a holistic concept that makes everyday life at school more sustainable? For example, we could set up recycling stations, suggest energy-saving measures and organize workshops for the students to learn how they can live in a more environmentally friendly way themselves."

There was silence in the group for a moment. Anna felt her insecurity returning. "Maybe that was too much," she thought, "maybe it wasn't good."

But then she saw how the other girls' eyes began to light up. "That's a really good idea, Anna!" Lisa exclaimed enthusiastically. "We could even do a presentation on how each class can reduce their ecological footprint."

"And we could involve the teachers," Johanna added. "Maybe we could also organize a project week about it."

Clara nodded in agreement. "That would be really cool. Anna, your idea will really help us."

Anna could hardly believe it. She had expected that her quiet nature and deep thoughts would not be well received, but instead her ideas had taken the group's project in a new direction. The other girls immediately began to discuss and develop her suggestions, and for the first time Anna really felt part of the team.

Over the following weeks, the group worked intensively on their project. Anna contributed more and more ideas, and the other girls appreciated her calm, thoughtful manner. They noticed that Anna often thought more deeply about things and suggested solutions that they would never have considered themselves. Anna's influence made the project one of the strongest in the class.

On the day of the presentation, Anna was nervous, but also proud. She had put her ideas on paper and was ready to present them to the class. As she stepped forward with her group, she could feel the eyes of the other students on her, but this time she didn't feel invisible. She knew she had something valuable to say.

Clara began the presentation and one by one the girls presented their ideas. When it was Anna's turn, she spoke calmly and clearly about the importance of sustainability in everyday school life and how her suggestions could be implemented. The class listened attentively and when she finished, there was appreciative applause.

After the presentation, Ms. Meier approached Anna and the other girls. "That was an impressive job you did," she said in praise. "And Anna, your ideas were really exceptional. You showed that it's not always the loudest who have the best ideas."

Anna felt her heart leap for joy. She had always thought that her quiet nature made her less valuable, but now she knew that the opposite was true. Her quietness was a strength that enabled her to think more deeply and find creative solutions.

On the way home, Anna told her mother about her success. "Mom, I think I've learned something important today," she said thoughtfully.

"And what would that be?" her mother asked curiously.

"That I don't have to be loud and sociable to be valuable. My quiet nature has its own power, and I can be proud of that."

Her mother smiled proudly. "That's a wonderful realization, Anna. You're just right the way you are, and it's nice to see that you see it that way now too."

Anna nodded and looked out of the window. The day that had started with so much uncertainty ended with a sense of pride and confidence. She knew that there would be many more days when she felt insecure, but she had learned something important: her uniqueness was her strength, and that made her special.

Anna has learned that her quiet and thoughtful nature is a strength. She has discovered that you don't have to be loud to be valuable and that quiet thoughts often produce the most profound ideas. You too should be proud of your uniqueness, whether you are loud or quiet, gregarious or reserved. Trust in your strengths and be proud of what makes you special - because you are just right the way you are.

You have everything you need inside you.

Leyla and the festival of cultures

Leyla stood at the window of her room and looked out onto the street. The children from her neighborhood were playing tag, laughing loudly, their cheerful shouts echoing up to her. But Leyla didn't feel like going outside. She had not yet made any real friends at her new school and often felt like an outsider. Her family had moved to Germany from another country a few years ago, and even though Leyla spoke the language well, there were times when she felt different - different, and sometimes alone.

Leyla loved her family and her culture, but it was sometimes difficult at school. Her classmates didn't understand her family's traditions, which often made her feel insecure. "Why can't I just be like the others?" she often asked herself. "Why do I always have to feel so strange?"

The next day at school there was a lot of excitement. Mrs. Weber, Leyla's class teacher, had an announcement to make. "We want to do something special this year," she said with a smile. "Our school is going to have a big party and each class will contribute to it. You have the freedom to choose the theme yourselves. What do you think we could do?"

The class immediately started making suggestions. "How about a sports tournament?" Tim suggested.

"Or we could put on a play," Clara added.

Leyla listened, but she didn't feel that she was being addressed. She had the feeling that her ideas weren't that important here, that she simply didn't belong. But while the others continued to discuss, a thought suddenly occurred to her. "What if we do something that brings us all together?" she thought. "Something that shows that it's okay to be different."

"I... I have an idea," Leyla finally said, her voice soft but firm.

The class fell silent and all eyes turned to her. "Yes, Leyla?" Mrs. Weber asked encouragingly.

Leyla felt her heart beating faster, but she forced herself to continue. "What if we organized a festival of cultures?" she suggested.

"Each of us could present the culture of our family, whether it's our own or one that interests us. We could wear traditional clothes, bring food from different countries and perform dances or music from different cultures."

There was silence for a moment, but then the other children began to nod and smile. "That's a great idea, Leyla!" exclaimed Clara enthusiastically. "We could learn so much about different cultures!"

"And we could also invite our parents, who might be able to help us," Tim added. "My grandma makes a super tasty Italian dish, for example."

Ms. Weber smiled at Leyla. "I think it's a wonderful idea," she said. "It would be a great opportunity to learn from each other and celebrate the diversity in our class. What do you think?"

The class agreed enthusiastically and Leyla felt a wave of relief spread through her. For the first time in a long time, she felt not only accepted, but also valued. Her idea had brought the class together and she was proud to celebrate her culture and that of her classmates.

Over the next few weeks, the class worked intensively on the preparations for the festival. Leyla was appointed coordinator of the project and she helped her classmates to organize their contributions. She herself planned to bring traditional dishes from her home country and perform a dance that her mother had taught her.

In the afternoons, Leyla often sat in the kitchen with her mother while they tried out the recipes. "I'm so proud of you, Leyla," said her mother one evening as they kneaded the dough for a special pastry together. "It's important that you don't forget your roots and that you're proud of where you come from."

Leyla smiled and felt her heart warm. "I'm afraid the others won't like the food or the dancing," she confessed quietly.

Her mother put a hand on her shoulder. "They'll like it because it comes from the heart," she said gently. "You're showing them a part of yourself, and that's the nicest thing you can do."

On the day of the celebration, the school was buzzing with excitement. The assembly hall was festively decorated and flags from different countries hung on the walls. Food from all over the world was laid out on long tables and the pupils wore traditional clothing or dressed in the colors of their home countries. It was a colorful and lively spectacle.

Leyla stood in the middle of the action and watched her classmates discussing the different cultures. She felt happy and content. Her idea had made the festival possible and she was proud that she had had the courage to share her idea.

When it was time for the performances, Leyla stepped in front of the class. She wore a traditional dress from her home country and explained the dance she was about to perform. Her voice trembled slightly, but she could feel the support of her class behind her.

Then the music started and Leyla danced. She let the music carry her and forgot everything around her for a moment. It was as if she felt a connection to her roots, a connection that made her strong and proud.

When the dance ended, loud applause broke out. Leyla blushed with joy and felt the warmth of recognition flood through her. Her classmates came up to her to congratulate her. "That was so nice, Leyla," Clara said, beaming. "You really made the party special."

"Thank you," Leyla replied quietly, but her heart was full of pride. She had realized that her difference was nothing to be ashamed of. On the contrary, it was something that enriched her and that she could share with others.

At the end of the day, as the festival drew to a close, Leyla stayed in the auditorium for a moment and looked at the empty tables and the colorful flags. She felt fulfilled and grateful. She knew that from now on she would always be proud of her culture and that she dared to be different. She had not only accepted her roots, but celebrated them - and that made her stronger than ever.

Leyla has learned that her origins and her cultural identity are something special that she doesn't have to hide. On the contrary, she has discovered that it is important to be proud of your own culture and to share it with others.

You too should be proud of your roots, no matter where you come from or what you look like. Your uniqueness is a strength that enriches the world - so celebrate it and be proud of who you are.

You are enough, just as you are.

Mara and the Magic of Technology

Mara sat in her father's garage and listened to the familiar sound of wrench meeting metal. The smell of oil and rubber was in the air, and the sound of machinery coming to life was music to her ears. Mara loved spending time with her father here, wrenching on cars and understanding how all the little parts worked together to create something big.

"Give me the pliers, Mara," said her father, reaching his hand over his shoulder. Mara grabbed the pliers and handed them to him with a smile. "Thank you, my darling. You really are a great help."

Mara felt her pride grow. It was a wonderful feeling to do something practical, something that not everyone could do. She loved technology and mechanics, the feeling that she could create or repair something with her hands. But as much as she enjoyed this time with her father, she also knew that her enthusiasm was not always met with understanding.

At school, Mara often felt like an outsider. While the other girls talked about fashion, music or movies, Mara thought about motors, gears and circuits. She knew she was different, and sometimes that was hard for her. There were days when she wondered if she should just hide her interests to fit in better.

"Why do you like that?" a girl in her class once asked when Mara was raving about a new engine that she and her father had installed. "That's not for girls. You should be more interested in normal things."

These words had affected Mara deeply, although she tried not to let it show. "What if they're right?" she sometimes asked herself. "What if I really am different and no one can understand that?"

But deep in her heart, Mara knew that her passion for technology was a part of her that she could not - and would not - give up.

One day, as Mara sat quietly in school as usual, trying not to pay too much attention to the conversations of her classmates, Mr. Schmidt, her science teacher, entered the room with a broad smile. "Today I have a special announcement," he said as he stood in front of the class. "This year we are going to do a special project. You will be working in groups to build a small robot. The team with the best robot will represent our school in a regional competition."

The class immediately began to murmur excitedly. Building a robot? That sounded interesting - and challenging. Mara felt her heart beat faster. A robot! That was exactly what she had been waiting for. Finally a project where she could show what she could really do.

When the groups were divided up, Mara ended up in a team with three other girls. Lisa, Clara and Nina were nice girls, but they were more interested in fashion and music than technology. "A robot?" Lisa said skeptically when she understood the task. "How are we supposed to manage that?"

"Yeah, I don't know anything about that," Clara added. "That sounds really difficult."

Mara felt a mixture of excitement and uncertainty spreading through her. She really wanted to take part and contribute her ideas, but she also knew that the other girls might not take her seriously. "Maybe I should just give it a go," she thought, "what have I got to lose?"

"Well... I might be able to help us," Mara said hesitantly. "I have a bit of experience with technology. My father and I often work together in the garage. We could build a simple robot that moves and maybe avoids a few obstacles."

The other girls looked at her in surprise. "Really?" asked Nina in disbelief. "You can do that?"

Mara nodded shyly. "Yes, I think so. We could at least try."

"That would be great," Lisa said and smiled. "I really have no idea where to start. If you can help us, that would be great."

Encouraged by the support of her teammates, Mara began to develop a plan. Over the next few days, the group met regularly and Mara showed the others how to assemble the parts and connect the circuits correctly. Although it was difficult at first, the girls quickly took a liking to the work and became interested in the technology.

"It's really fun," said Clara one day as they were attaching the wires to the motors together. "I never thought I'd be doing something so cool."

Mara smiled proudly. It was good to see her classmates enjoying creating something. And even better was the feeling that she could finally share her passion for technology with others without having to be ashamed of it.

On the day of the presentation, the class was full of anticipation. All the teams presented their robots, and when it was Mara's group's turn, she suddenly felt insecure again. "What if our robot doesn't work?" she thought nervously, "What if the others don't like it?"

But when she placed the robot on the table and activated the circuit, the small device began to move and skillfully avoid obstacles. The class burst into applause and Mara felt her insecurity evaporate. She had done it. Her robot worked perfectly and she could see the excitement on her classmates' faces.

"That's incredible, Mara!" exclaimed Nina, clapping her hands enthusiastically. "You really helped us to pull this off. We could never have done it without you."

Mara could no longer suppress her smile. "Thank you," she said quietly, but inside she felt stronger and more confident than ever.

When Mr. Schmidt finally announced the winners of the competition and Mara's team took first place, the joy was overwhelming. They had made it - not only because of the robot, but also because of the teamwork and determination they had shown together.

Mara has learned that her enthusiasm for technology is something she doesn't have to hide. She has discovered that it's okay to be different and to have interests that not everyone shares. You too should be proud of your passions, no matter how unusual they may seem. Trust in your strengths and be proud of what makes you tick - because you are just right the way you are.

You make the world a better place in your own way.

Clara finds her inner strength

Clara sat alone in her room and stared at the book lying on the desk in front of her. It was one of those books that the teacher had recommended to learn more about role models - people who had achieved great things, who were courageous and had changed the world. Clara leafed listlessly through the pages and felt the doubt rising in her. "Why should I even read this?" she thought, "I'm not really good at anything."

Clara was a quiet girl. She hardly stood out at school, she had no special talents and often felt invisible. Her classmates had their own strengths - some were good at sport, others at art or music. But Clara didn't know what she was good at. She had the feeling that she was only mediocre at everything, never outstanding.

"Maybe I'm just not special," she thought sadly. These thoughts were like a shadow that constantly hung over her and prevented her from feeling really good about herself. She often doubted herself and her worth. "Why can't I be as talented or brave as the others?" she often asked herself.

At school, the teachers noticed that Clara was reserved, but no one really knew how to help her. Clara didn't know either. She wanted to belong, but she didn't know how. She wanted to feel valuable, but she didn't know why she didn't.

One day, Mrs. Meier, Clara's class teacher, gave the class a new task. "We're going to do a book project over the next few weeks," she explained. "Each of you will read a book about a role model and then give a short presentation about it. It's important that you choose someone who inspires you and who shows you what you can achieve with inner strength."

Clara felt a knot forming in her stomach. A presentation? About a role model? "That's not for me," she thought immediately. "What if I can't find anyone to inspire me?"

The next day, Clara went to the library and looked for a book she could read. She felt lost among all the shelves full of stories about people who were brave and strong, who had achieved great things. But suddenly she stopped in front of a book whose title piqued her curiosity: "The Heroine from the Shadows". It was the story of a young woman who had remained brave and strong during a difficult time, even though she often felt weak and insecure.

"Maybe I'll find something here that can help me," thought Clara and took the book home with her.

At home, she sat down in her bed, snuggled up in her blanket and began to read. The story of the heroine who made her way despite all adversity immediately captivated Clara. This woman had never seen herself as anything special, but she had always believed in what she was doing. She had found her inner strength, not because she was particularly talented or brave, but because she had never given up believing in herself.

The more Clara read, the more she felt connected to the heroine. "Maybe I'm stronger than I think, too," she thought. "Maybe true strength doesn't come from being particularly talented, but from just getting on with it, even when it's hard."

Over the next few days, Clara began to think about herself. She wondered why she had always doubted herself. She had always thought that she was nothing special, but maybe she just hadn't realized what her true strength was. Maybe it was her ability to listen, her patience or her kindness - things she had never seen as special talents before.

As the day of the presentation approached, Clara was nervous, but also excited. She had decided to talk about the heroine from her book and how this woman had inspired her to believe in herself. "I can do this," she kept telling herself. "I have something important to say."

On the day of the presentation, Clara stood in front of the class and felt her heart beating faster. But as she began to speak, she felt her insecurities slowly disappear. She talked about the heroine who never gave up and how she had learned to appreciate her own strengths. "True strength doesn't come from the outside," she finally said. "It comes from within. And I believe that each of us has this strength within us."

When Clara had finished, there was silence for a moment before the class burst into applause. Mrs. Meier stepped up to her and smiled. "That was a wonderful presentation, Clara," she said. "You showed us all how important it is to believe in yourself."

Clara felt a wave of relief and pride spread through her. She had made it. She had found her voice and realized that she was worth more than she had ever thought. From that day on, Clara began to see herself through different eyes. She knew that she might not be the best at everything, but she had an inner strength that would carry her through anything.

Clara has learned that true strength does not come from outside, but from within. She has discovered that she is much more valuable and stronger than she ever thought. You too should always believe that you are special, regardless of how others see you. Your inner strength is your greatest power - trust it and be proud of what makes you special. Because you are just right the way you are.

Your inner strength makes you special.

Stay true to yourself

As you have read the stories in this book, you have seen that each girl has gone her own way - with all her insecurities, fears and challenges. But in the end, each of them has realized something important: Their uniqueness is their greatest strength.

You too have your very own talents, dreams and characteristics that make you special. Sometimes it can be difficult to accept yourself, especially if you feel that you are different. But it is precisely these differences that make you valuable and unique.

Take these stories with you as a reminder that you should never stop believing in yourself. No matter what others say or think - you are exactly right the way you are. Stay true to yourself, because that is your true strength.

Always remember: Your uniqueness is a gift, and the world needs exactly what you have to offer.

Printed in Great Britain
by Amazon

51761229R00053